Stewart

by John Mackay

Lang**Syne**

PUBLISHING

WRITING *to* REMEMBER

LangSyne
PUBLISHING
WRITING *to* REMEMBER

Vineyard Business Centre,
Pathhead, Midlothian EH37 5XP
Tel: 01875 321 203 Fax: 01875 321 233
E-mail: info@lang-syne.co.uk
www.langsyneshop.co.uk

Design by Dorothy Meikle
Printed by Ricoh Print Scotland
© Lang Syne Publishers Ltd 2011

ISBN 978-1-85217-055-4

Stewart

SEPT NAMES INCLUDE:

APPIN:
Carmichael
Combich
Levack
Livingstone
MacCombich
MacKinlay
MacLay
MacMichael

ROYAL LINE
SEPTS:
Boyd
France
Garrow
Lennox
Monteith

ATHOLL:
Crookshanks
Cruickshanks
Duilach
Gray,
McGlashan

BUTE:
Bannatyne
Fullerton
Jameson
Jamieson
MacCamie
MacCaw
MacCloy
MacKirdy
MacLewis
MacMunn
MacMutrie

VIRESCIT VULNERE VIRTUS

Stewart

MOTTO:
Virescit vulnere virtus
(Courage grows strong at a wound).

CREST:
The Oak and the thistle.

TERRITORY:
Appin, Balquhidder, Bute and Arran, areas
of Atholl including Grandtully, Garth Castle
and Balnakeilly, areas around Loch Katrine,
Loch Voil and Loch Earn including
Ardvorlich, are south-east of Callander
including Doune Castle, around Elgin.

Chapter one:

The origins of the clan system

by Rennie McOwan

The original Scottish clans of the Highlands and the great families of the Lowlands and Borders were gatherings of families, relatives, allies and neighbours for mutual protection against rivals or invaders.

Scotland experienced invasion from the Vikings, the Romans and English armies from the south. The Norman invasion of what is now England also had an influence on land-holding in Scotland. Some of these invaders stayed on and in time became 'Scottish'.

The word clan derives from the Gaelic language term 'clann', meaning children, and it was first used many centuries ago as communities were formed around tribal lands in glens and mountain fastnesses.

The format of clans changed over the centuries, but at its best the chief and his family held the land on behalf of all, like trustees, and the ordinary clansmen and women believed they had a blood relationship with the founder of their clan.

There were two way duties and obligations. An inadequate chief could be deposed and replaced by someone of greater ability.

Clan people had an immense pride in race. Their relationship with the chief was like adult children to a father and they had a real dignity.

The concept of clanship is very old and a more feudal notion of authority gradually crept in.

Pictland, for instance, was divided into seven principalities ruled by feudal leaders who were the strongest and most charismatic leaders of their particular groups.

By the sixth century the 'British' kingdoms of Strathclyde, Lothian and Celtic Dalriada (Argyll) had emerged and Scotland, as one nation, began to take shape in the time of King Kenneth MacAlpin.

Some chiefs claimed descent from

ancient kings which may not have been accurate in every case.

By the twelfth and thirteenth centuries the clans and families were more strongly brought under the central control of Scottish monarchs.

Lands were awarded and administered more and more under royal favour, yet the power of the area clan chiefs was still very great.

The long wars to ensure Scotland's independence against the expansionist ideas of English monarchs extended the influence of some clans and reduced the lands of others.

Those who supported Scotland's greatest king, Robert the Bruce, were awarded the territories of the families who had opposed his claim to the Scottish throne.

In the Scottish Borders country - the notorious Debatable Lands - the great families built up a ferocious reputation for providing war-like men accustomed to raiding into England and occasionally fighting one another.

Chiefs had the power to dispense justice

and to confiscate lands and clan warfare produced a society where martial virtues - courage, hardiness, tenacity - were greatly admired.

Gradually the relationship between the clans and the Crown became strained as Scottish monarchs became more orientated to life in the Lowlands and, on occasion, towards England.

The Highland clans spoke a different language, Gaelic, whereas the language of Lowland Scotland and the court was Scots and in more modern times, English.

Highlanders dressed differently, had different customs, and their wild mountain land sometimes seemed almost foreign to people living in the Lowlands.

It must be emphasised that Gaelic culture was very rich and story-telling, poetry, piping, the clarsach (harp) and other music all flourished and were greatly respected.

Highland culture was different from other parts of Scotland but it was not inferior or less sophisticated.

Central Government, whether in London

"The spirit of the clan means much to thousands of people".

or Edinburgh, sometimes saw the Gaelic clans as a challenge to their authority and some sent expeditions into the Highlands and west to crush the power of the Lords of the Isles.

Nevertheless, when the eighteenth century Jacobite Risings came along the cause of the Stuarts was mainly supported by Highland clans.

The word Jacobite comes from the Latin for James - Jacobus. The Jacobites wanted to restore the exiled Stuarts to the throne of Britain.

The monarchies of Scotland and England became one in 1603 when King James VI of Scotland (1st of England) gained the English throne after Queen Elizabeth died.

The Union of Parliaments of Scotland and England, the Treaty of Union, took place in 1707.

Some Highland clans, of course, and Lowland families opposed the Jacobites and supported the incoming Hanoverians.

After the Jacobite cause finally went down at Culloden in 1746 a kind of ethnic cleansing took place. The power of the chiefs was curtailed. Tartan and the pipes were banned in law.

Many emigrated, some because they wanted to, some because they were evicted by force. In addition, many Highlanders left for the cities of the south to seek work.

Many of the clan lands became home to sheep and deer shooting estates.

But the warlike traditions of the clans and the great Lowland and Border families lived on, with their descendants fighting bravely for freedom in two world wars.

Remember the men from whence you came, says the Gaelic proverb, and to that could be added the role of many heroic women.

The spirit of the clan, of having roots, whether Highland or Lowland, means much to thousands of people.

A map of the clans' homelands.

Chapter two:

A bloody birth

Almost every branch of the Stewart family has in their coat of arms a sign that looks like a section of a chessboard, black and white square or 'dices' similar to those currently seen of the caps of policemen.

This heraldic device originated in the cloth board on which accountants worked out the revenues due the treasury which was similar to that used in chess or chequers (hence the term Chancellor of the Exchequer).

The chief accountant to the Scottish King was called the High Steward and it is from this title that the clan name derives.

The High Stewardship of Scotland was made a hereditary appointment in the 12th century and the family of one Walter Fitz Alan took the device into their coat-of-arms.

This Walter was descended from an Earl of Brittany who came over with William the

Conqueror in the Norman invasion of 1066 but who, later in his career and for some reason now lost in the mists of time, "incurred the displeasure of the Conqueror" and so retired to Scotland where David 1st used his expertise by appointing him Royal Steward.

The High Steward was more than just a counter of coins, however, since he was also quite capable of raising and even leading into battle an army on behalf of his King.

Walter the High Steward claimed descent from Banquo, Thane of Lochaber, and through him to the ancient kings of Scotland.

Banquo was murdered by Macbeth but his son Fleance escaped and fled to Wales where he fell in love with a princess and made his rivals so jealous that they killed him.

His son Walter in turn fled overseas (murder and flight seemed to be a constant theme in the early Stewart history) and took refuge at the court of Alan the Red of Brittany and it was there that, in gratitude for the protection he had received, he took the name Fitz Alan ('fitz' being in Welsh the same as Mac, or son of, in Scotland).

It was this Walter who came over with the Normans and founded the Stewart dynasty in this country when he came north.

Gradually over the years the Stewart family had many branches and cadet houses and produced five earls – Angus, Lennox, Menteith, Buchan, Traquair – and many other powerful leaders.

The sixth High Steward, also called Walter, gave support to Robert the Bruce during the Wars of Independence and duly married King Robert's daughter Marjorie.

Their son became Robert II and thus the Royal line was established.

Chapter three:

A dynasty is born

The dynasty continued throughout Scottish and British history, either on the throne or fighting to reclaim it, up to 1746, its two most famous members being Mary, Queen of Scots and Bonnie Prince Charlie.

Another Stewart of distinction was King Robert III's son the Duke of Albany although his character was marred by strong streaks of deviousness and ruthlessness.

When his father died, he acted as Regent and had his eye on the throne when his nephew James succeeded but was not crowned, being made a prisoner in England after being captured on his way to France to advance his youthful education.

When David, Duke of Rothesay, was made Regent, Albany was later suspected of arranging his murder and he also contrived to delay the negotiations with England regarding the return of the young James 1st.

When Albany died, still lording it over Scotland, he was succeeded by his son Murdach who arranged for the rightful return to the throne of James and the King duly arrived in his kingdom with his bride, the lovely Joanna Beaufort.

But James was less than gracious to his benefactor and took a wholesale revenge on the whole Albany family, including Murdach. There were mass executions of all their branches and followers on Heading Hill near Stirling.

By the 14th century the Stewart clan had spread northwards into the Highlands and not all of them were welcomed.

For instance, King Robert III's youngest brother Alexander was colloquially known as the Wolf of Badenoch which captures succinctly his psychopathic talents for pillaging, plundering and recklessly murdering throughout his own northern territories. He deserted his wife in 1389 and was excommunicated by the Bishops of Moray and Ross. This meant little to the Wolf yet he was annoyed enough to burn to the ground the grand

Cathedral of Elgin which had been one of the gothic glories of medieval Scotland. Its gaunt, broken remains still bear witness to its ancient grandeur and foul desecration.

Many of the Aberdeenshire, Moray and Banff Stewarts are descended from the illegitimate sons of the Wolf (although they would be loathe to admit it) since, among his many other sins, he was good at spreading his seed throughout his lands.

King James I turned his attentions to the ever turbulent Highlands, which many of his kinsmen including the Wolf, were keeping in a state of constant unrest. He invited the rebellious, independent-minded chiefs to a Parliament in Inverness but as each chief arrived they were arrested and thrown into a dungeon. The King, who was also a poet, took pen in hand to record the occasion with the couthy lines –

> *'To the dungeons strong*
> *Haul the wretches along,*
> *As in Christ's my hope,*
> *They deserve the rope.'*

They did not all get the rope, however, Some were beheaded and others exiled abroad. These were typical draconian methods the Stewarts used to retain their tight, steely grip on their violent kingdom.

James made many enemies among his barons and in 1437, when staying at the Blackfriars Monastery at Perth, he was chatting to his wife and her ladies-in-waiting prior to going to bed when he heard the clashing sound of approaching men-at-arms in the torchlit dark and the gruff shouts of men searching the premises. This sent him down a trap door in an attempt to escape while Lady Catherine Douglas thrust her arm into the metal brackets at the main door designed to take a locking bar but the delay proved futile and James was duly stabbed to death in an underground passage.

But such was the uproar over this assassination that the murderers had to flee into the wilds. When they were eventually caught, they were tortured and finally executed over three excruciating days.

When James II ascended the throne, he made the city of Edinburgh the capital of his realm because he had spent many happy childhood hours getting an education there. He caused the first town wall to be built in its defence and made many other improvements including design innovations at the Royal Palace of Holyrood.

Another building closely associated with the Stewarts is Castle Stalker set on an islet in the Firth of Lorne in Appin. This was the stronghold of the Stewart Lords of Lorne and was later used as a hunting lodge by the Scottish Royalty.

In 1457 King James II granted the Earldom of Atholl to the Black Knight of Lorne, Sir James Stewart, an energetic and brilliant soldier who commanded the Royal army in its defeat of the Lord of the Isles, a pompus baron who considered himself and his subjects in the Hebrides to be outwith the rule of the Scottish Kings.

King James was, however, a violent tempered man who had stabbed to death an Earl of

Douglas (the Douglases being a constant menace to the Crown). He was killed when he stood too near a cannon which exploded during a siege in the Borders.

Chapter four:

A new force

James III proved himself a forceful, dynamic, progressive ruler, giving government posts not to nobles as had been the usual practice but to architects and other capable and practical working Scots of that time which did not appeal to the titled men at all.

He married the daughter of King Christian of Scandinavia who promised to give the Scottish king a grand dowry to mark the occasion but, before that could become a financial fact, James was prepared to accept the Orkneys and Shetlands as surety against its eventual arrival. After waiting four years, however, with no dowry in sight, James annexed the islands as part of his kingdom.

When, despite his constant strivings for peace, war broke out with England, he headed south to the Borders, not realising that his disgruntled nobles, fed up with his meritocracy, were

plotting with the enemy. The result was a ferocious battle after which James was murdered by
one of his foes who pretended to be a priest taking
him to shelter in a nearby mill.

The fourth James was reputedly the greatest Stewart of all. Tales have come down of his
ability to spring onto his horse without the aid of
a stirrup and, more practically, that he learned
Gaelic so that he could easier get to know and
confer with his unruly Highlanders – certainly he
invaded the Hebrides six times before he had
reconquered that area for the Crown, several
chieftains only saving their skins by joining
monasteries.

James also founded Colleges of Surgeons
in Edinburgh and Aberdeen and in 1507 encour-
aged two merchants to set up the first printing
press in Scotland.

He also built up the navy and renewed
'the Auld Alliance' with France and it was to support the latter that he declared war on England's
Henry VIII and crossed the Tweed, fatally posi-
tioning his army at Flodden.

As the English force moved into a position between the Scots and the Tweed, thus preventing retreat back into their own country, his master gunner pleaded with him to open fire while the enemy was strung out on the march but the King, being chivalrous to a fault, turned down this opportunity to strike a decisive blow. Another theory about the King was that his one true love, a Princess in Dunblane, had been poisoned by his barons as part of their political power play and James had a death wish at the ensuing battle (just like centuries later it was believed his descendant Charles Edward Stuart had a death wish at Culloden).

Whatever the reasons for the lack of proper generalship, the Scottish forces were also decimated by a new English weapon – the billhook, a long spear with a hook and axe that cut down the spears of the opposing infantry. As the English forces closed in and the blood red sun set on the massacre of Flodden Field, the slaughter resulted in the deaths of the King, three Bishops, thirteen earls and numerous other nobles.

The fifth James was a very human character who liked to go about his realm in disguise, the better to find out on the ground what exactly was going on.

While idling at Cramond Brig waiting on a farm girl, he was set on by the girl's official sweetheart and some supporters. The shouts and clashes were heard by Jock Howieson who was working with a flail threshing corn in a field by the river and, seeing that the odds were stacked unfavourably, he decided to join in and the attackers fled before his ferocious onslaught.

James, his identity unknown to Jock, thanked his rescuer and told him that next time he was in Edinburgh to call at Holyrood Palace where he would receive a reward. The King duly warned his staff of the coming caller who, when he arrived, was told to his delighted astonishment that he was being given the lands of Braehead near Cramond Brig – on condition that when the Scottish monarch passed that way he would be given refreshment as had been done by Jock to James after his rescue.

As late as 1927, the Howieson-Crawfurds of Braehead attended to the needs of King George V on his way north to Balmoral. On the death of James VI and 1st of Britain (the first Stewart to rule following the Union of Crowns in 1603), the reigns of Charles I and II were marked by bitter civil wars following religious disputes over forms of worship (the Stewarts remaining staunchly Catholic throughout the storms of the Protestant Reformation).

Stewart clansmen fought for the Marquis of Montrose in his campaigns against forces opposing the Stewart Kings and took part in what has been considered the most remarkable military strategic move ever achieved in Britain when, as the Marquis's forces were heading north and nearing the head of the Great Glen on their way to Inverness, word was brought that a Government army against the King was at Inverlochy to the south and confident that in the severe winter weather they would be safe from any Royalist attack. Montrose thought otherwise. He did an about turn, coming down with his men, not along the base of the glen where detection of his moves by government spies was always possible, but through the snow-deep wastes along the mountain heights, skirting the bulk of Ben Nevis itself, to appear to a surprised enemy and to win a devastating victory.

The lack of diplomacy and their inborn stubbornness and arrogance cost the Stewarts the throne of Britain when they refused to accommodate any of the reforming ideas coming to the fore.

Matters came to a head when King James II had to flee the country and the Protestant King William of Orange was invited to rule.

The Stewarts and their namesake followers were, of course, highly active in both the 1715 and 1745 Jacobite Rebllions aimed at putting first the Old Pretender and then his son back on the British throne.

But all their attempts ended in failure, the climactic defeat happening on the bloodsoaked moor at Culloden.

The Stewart clan standard was borne by a series of Highlanders during this battle who successively fell, mortally wounded, until it was lifted high by an Appin man called Donald. He realised all was lost, tore the silken yellow saltire cross on an azure background from its staff and, wrapping the emblem round his body, fought a ferocious rearguard solo action then escaped from the moor and his pursuers. He made it successfully to the safekeeping of Stewart of Ballachulish and it remained in the family until 1931 when it was formally given to the Stewart Society.

It was eventually presented to the United Services Museum in Edinburgh Castle at a ceremony attended by the descendants of Stewarts who had fought at Culloden.

Even when the '45 was over the Stewarts still suffered because when Colin Roy Campbell of Glen Ure – known as the Red Fox – was on his way to evict the Appin Stewarts from their forfeited lands he was shot off his horse and killed. James Stewart of the Glens, who was related to Ardsheal, the chief, was arrested and later tried and hanged for the murder although he was innocent. An example to others was needed. A monument to him stands on a knoll at the left hand side of the Ballachulish road bridge. The Appin murder has remained a mystery to this day and Robert Louis Stevenson incorporated it in his novel 'Kidnapped' where he gives this description of the chief suspect and his central character, Allan Breck Stewart, which was no doubt typical of many a Stewart in the heather over the years –

'He was smallish in stature, but well set up and as nimble as a goat; his face was of a good open expression, but sunburnt very dark, and heavily freckled and pitted with the smallpox; his eyes were unusually light and had a kind of dancing madness in them, that was both engaging and alarming; and when he took off his great-coat, he laid a pair of fine silver-mounted pistols on the table, and I saw that he was belted with a great sword. His manners, besides, were elegant, and he pledged the captain handsomely. Altogether I thought of him, at the first sight, that here was a man I would rather call my friend than my enemy'.

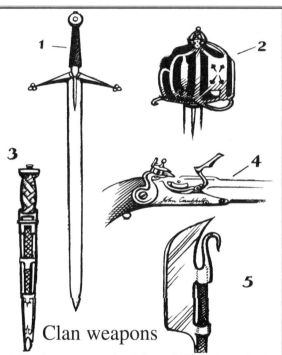

Clan weapons

1) The claymore or two-handed sword *(fifteenth or early six-teenth century)*
2) Basket hilt of broadsword made in Stirling, 1716
3) Highland dirk *(eighteenth century)*
4) Steel pistol *(detail)* made in Doune
5) Head of Lochaber Axe as carried in the '45 and earlier